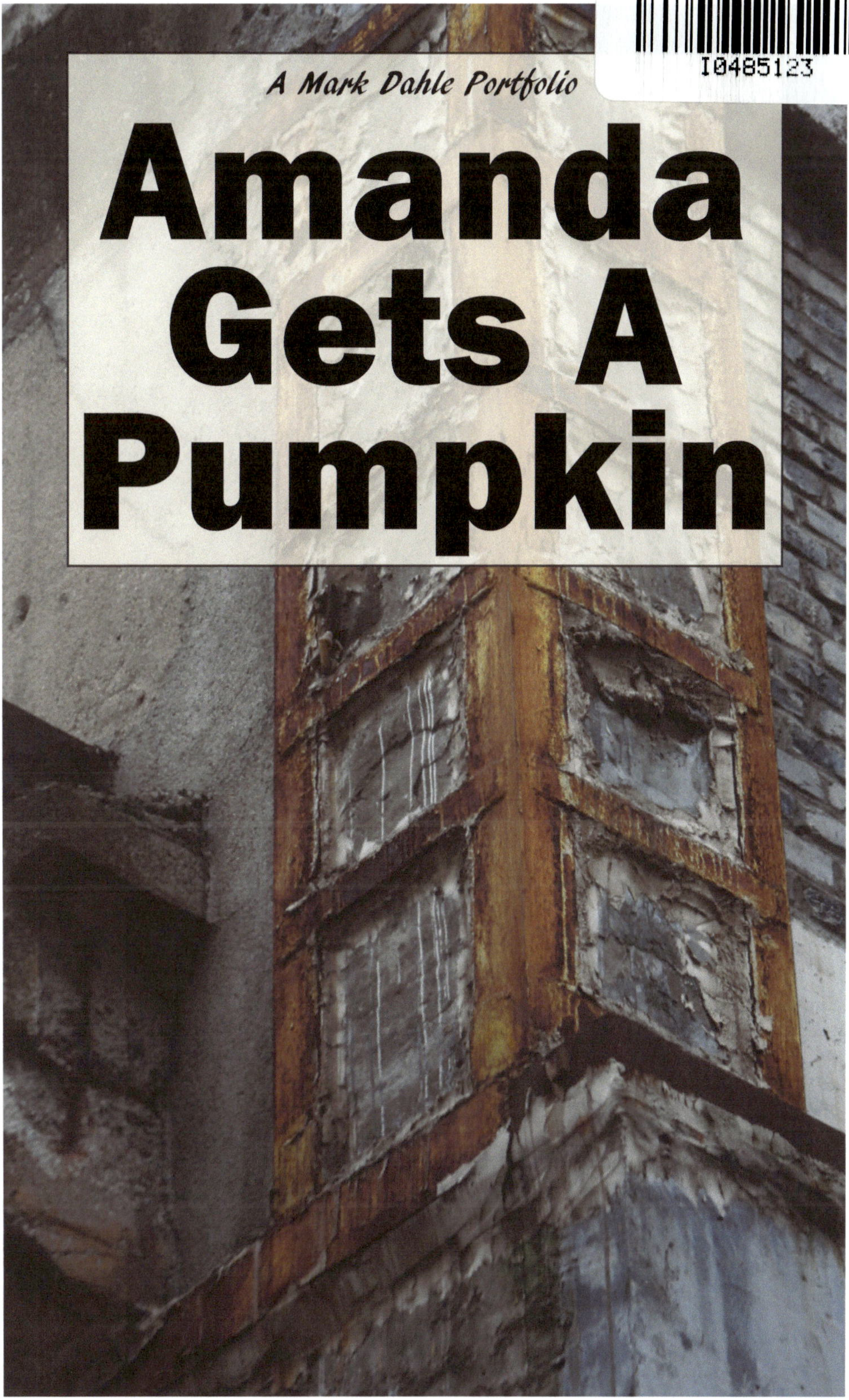

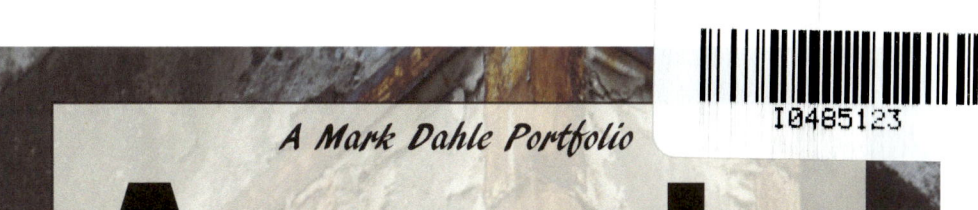

A Mark Dahle Portfolio

Amanda Gets A Pumpkin

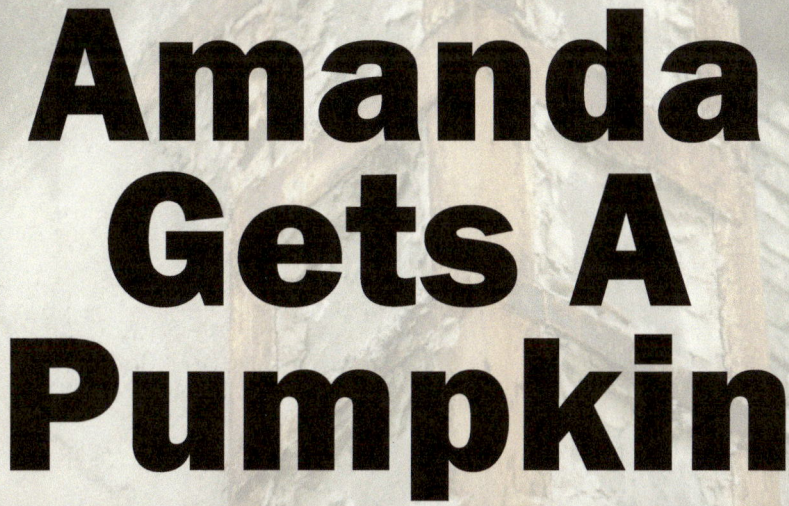

For Jojo.

~ ~ ~

Mark Dahle Portfolios can be read in a few minutes and enjoyed for a lifetime.

Unlike many picture books, the text in this book is not related to the art. This might seem weird at first. One thing that makes it better is to order more portfolios until you get used to it. Fortunately, space is provided on the pages for you to draw your own pictures of pumpkins if you like.

This portfolio includes a beautiful 36 x 24 inch painting (at the right), twenty-four great photos from Beijing, Xian and Shanghai, and a story about Amanda, who wanted a miracle.

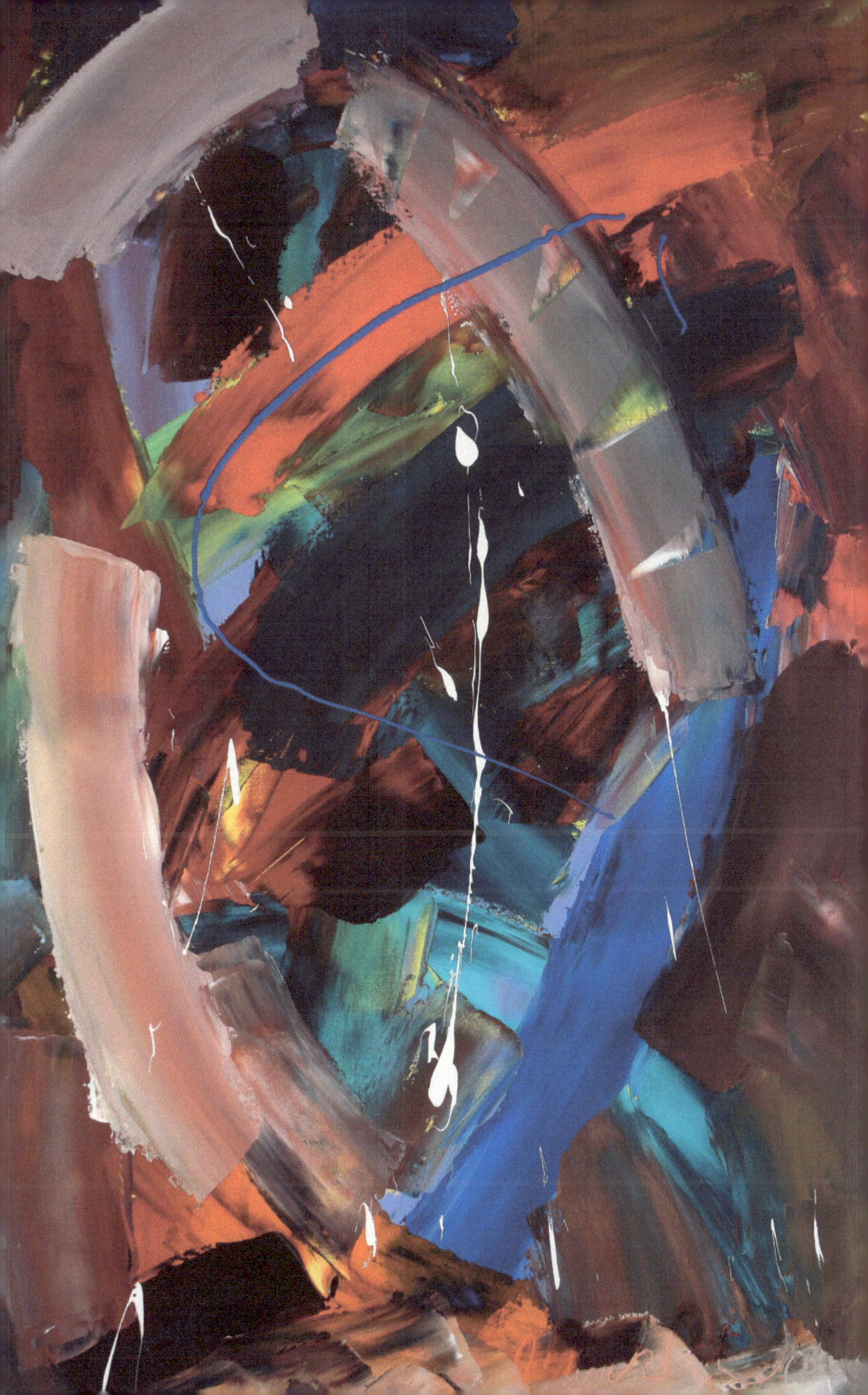

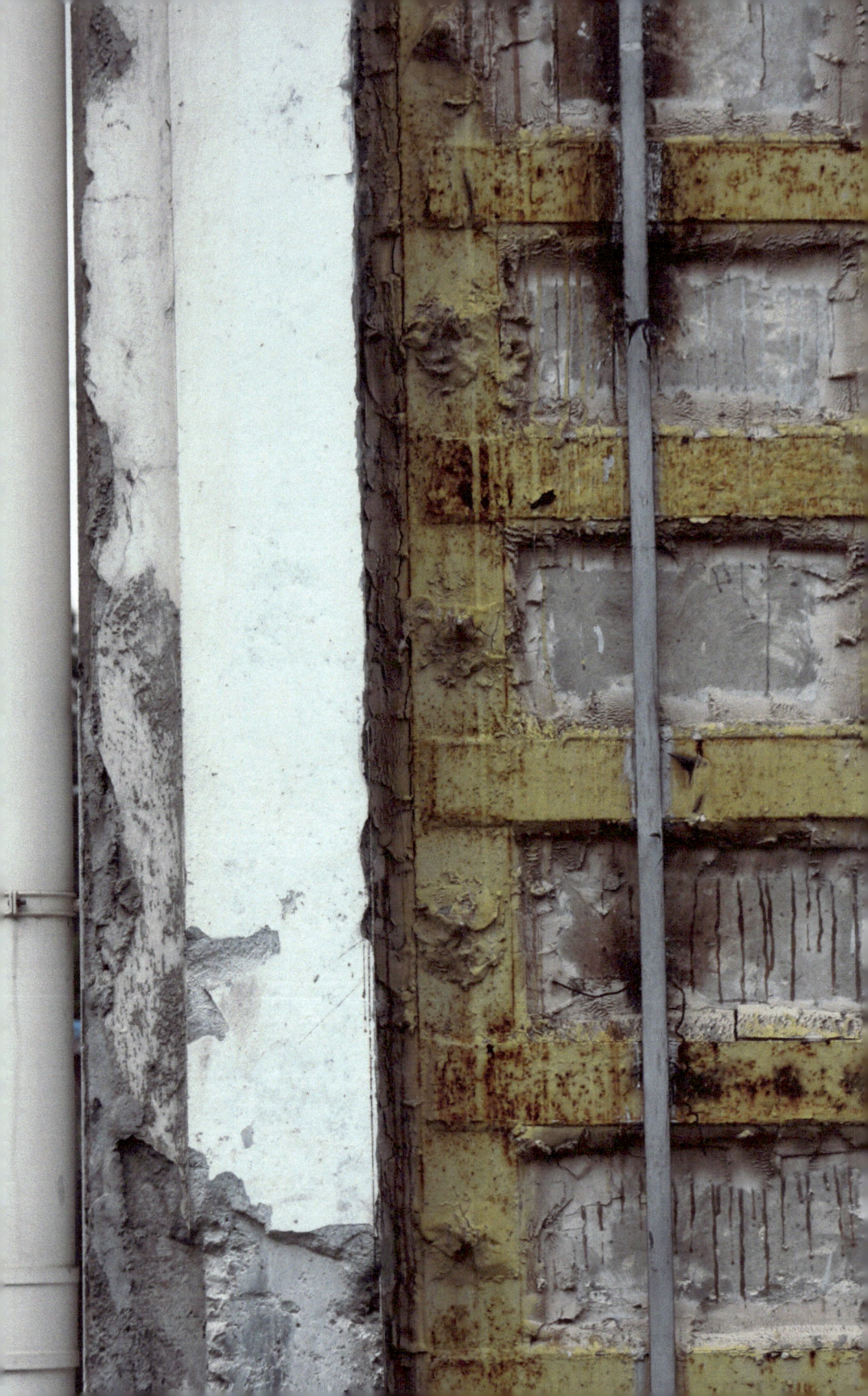

Amanda wanted a miracle. She squinted her eyes and curled her toes and imagined it was right in front of her.

But when she opened her eyes, nothing had happened.

Now what?

She didn't know.

For three days, Amanda tried everything she could think of. She said "Abracadabra" and waved a stick in the air. She tried commanding her miracle to happen, loudly, while standing on a chair. She made faces and pouted. She pleaded and smiled sweetly. She ran around the yard screaming. She laid on her bed at night, exhausted. While on her bed, she looked out the window, saw a star, and wished on it. Hard. She really wanted a miracle.

But at the end of the three days, nothing had happened.

Now what?

She didn't know.

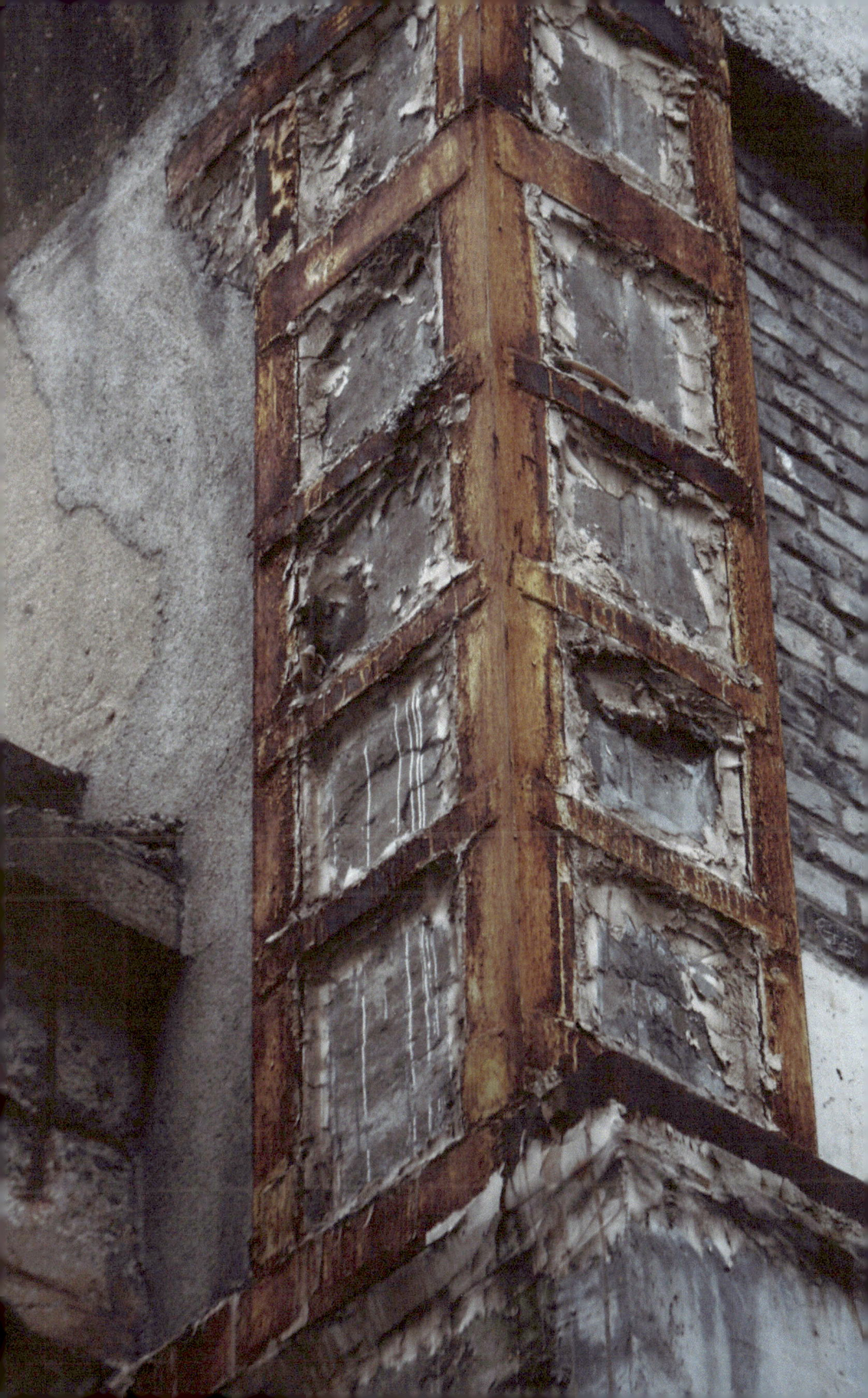

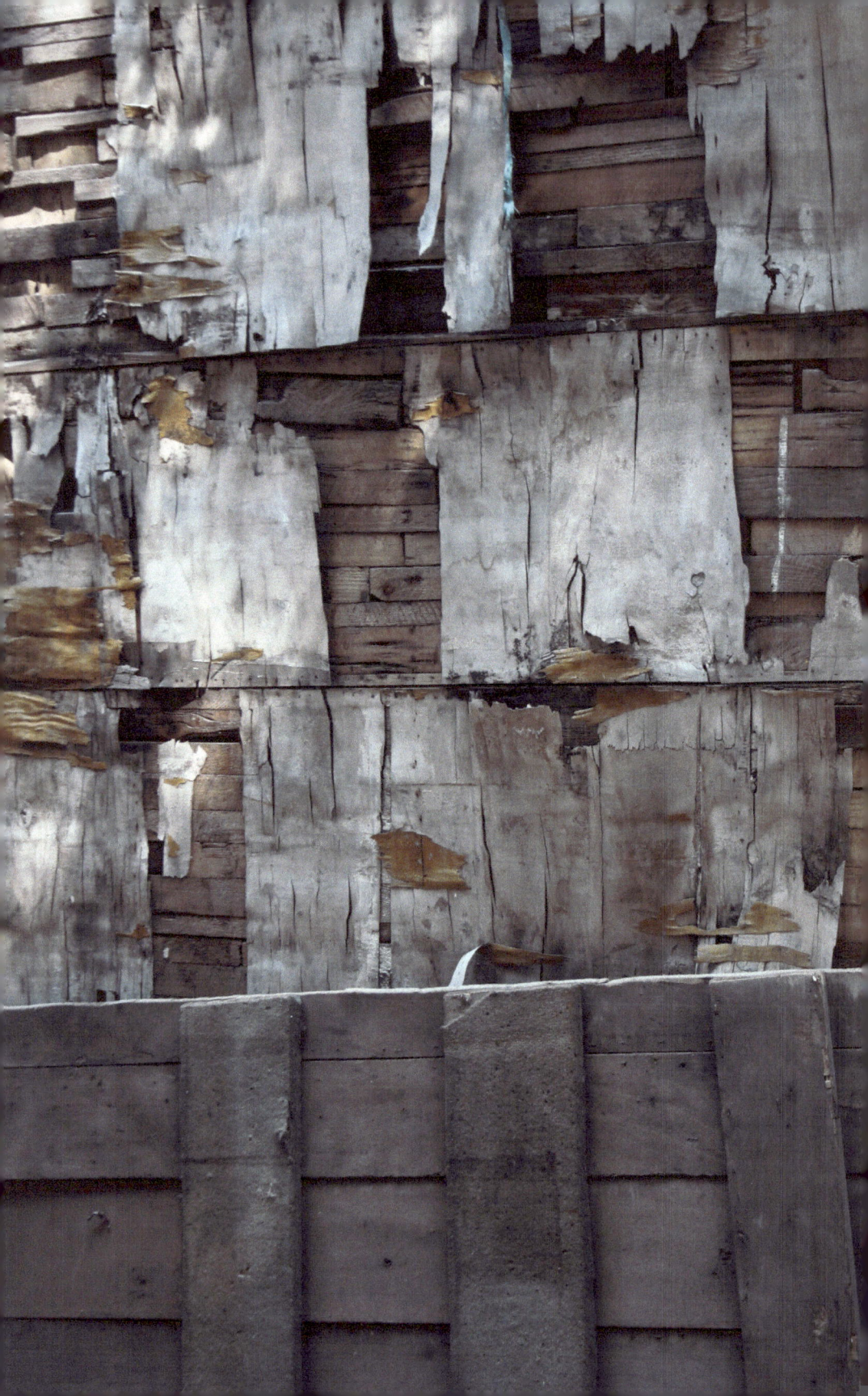

On the fourth day, her grandmother showed up.

Her grandmother knew everything. Maybe her grandmother could show her how to get a miracle. So Amanda asked.

"Oh!" said her grandmother, her big eyes twinkling. "I can show you that! Close your eyes and hold out your hands."

Amanda shut her eyes tight and held out her hands. Suddenly she was holding something that was *very* heavy.

She opened one eye to peek. It was a pumpkin! A bright orange pumpkin. It was so heavy she almost dropped it.

"There!" said her grandmother. "That should do it!"

Amanda opened both eyes. "It's a pumpkin," she said.

"Yes, dear."

"It's – ." Amanda paused. She didn't want to disappoint her grandmother. "It's very nice," she said. "And orange. A very pretty color. I like how round it is. I like the stem a lot, too. It's cute. But," she said, putting the pumpkin down on the ground, "I really wanted a miracle."

"Oh dear," said her grandmother. "You didn't want a pumpkin? Perhaps we'll have to try again. Close your eyes and hold out your hands."

Amanda shut her eyes and held out her hands and smiled. *This* time she'd get her miracle!

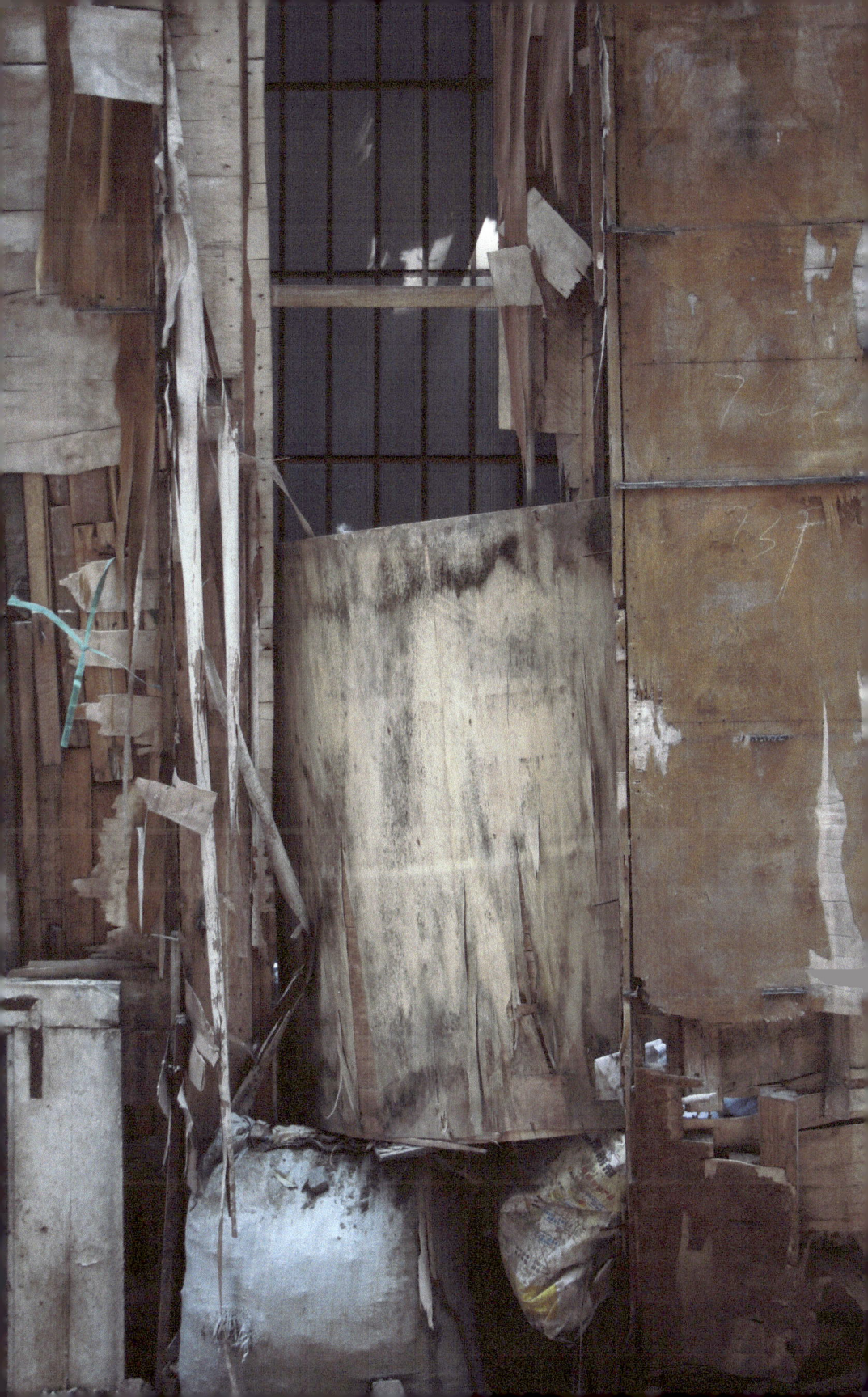

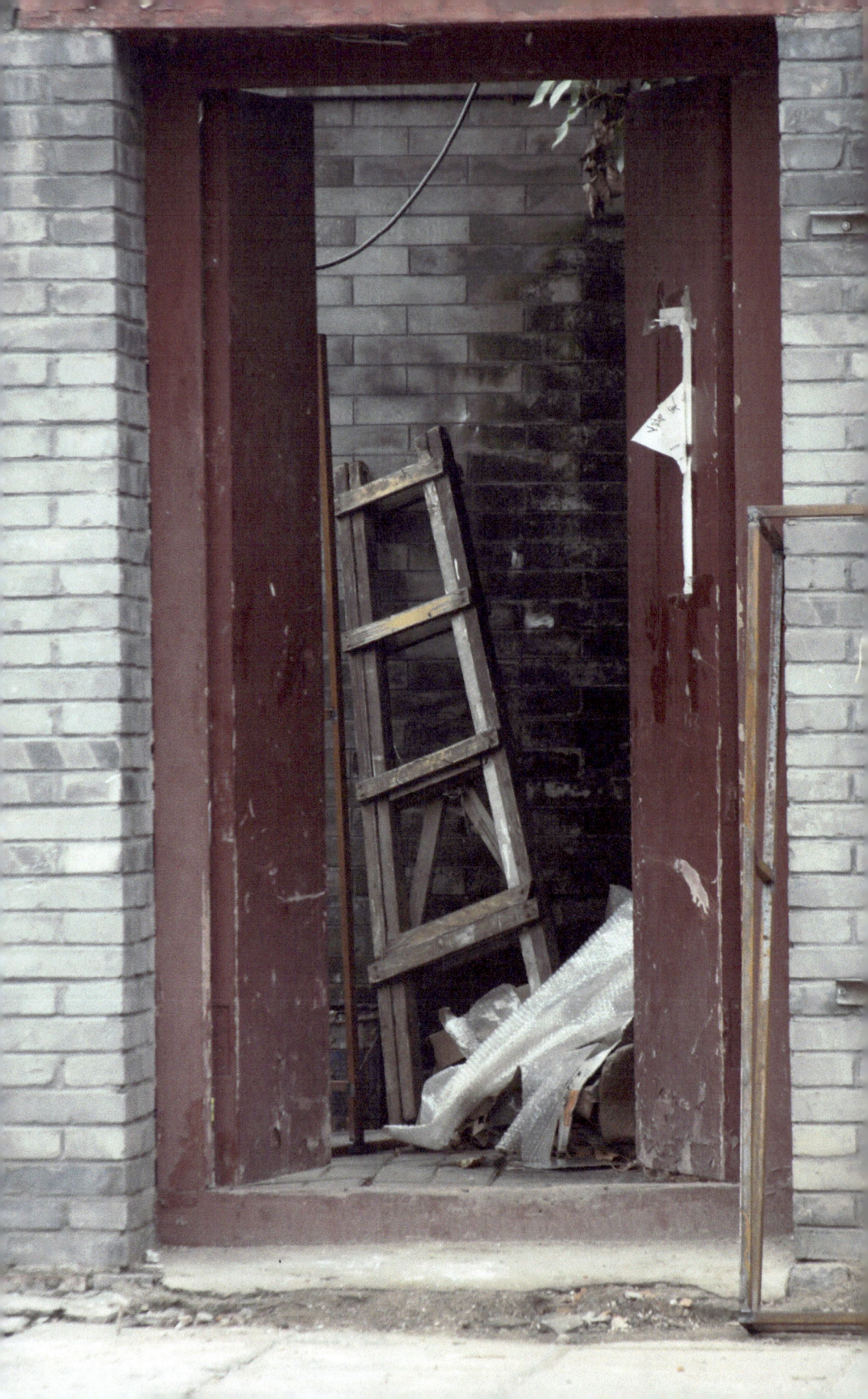

Amanda felt something light drop into her left hand. It was so light she barely felt it. She opened one eye to peek. In her hand were three seeds. Pumpkin seeds, if she guessed right.

"There!" said her grandmother. "That should do it!"

Amanda opened her eyes. "It looks like seeds," she said.

"Yes, dear," said her grandmother, beaming.

"They're very nice," Amanda said. "Not too heavy. Kind of light and all. They're a very pretty color – a nice pale yellow. I like their shape. But I really wanted a miracle."

"Oh dear," said her grandmother. "You didn't want pumpkin seeds? Are you sure?"

Amanda nodded. Her grandmother sighed. "Perhaps we'll have to try again."

Amanda's grandmother took her out to the garden. They found a patch that wasn't being used.

"First, we're going to pull up all the weeds," she said. "And right now, everything you see growing in this patch is a weed."

They both pulled weeds for quite a while. At last her grandmother straightened up. Slowly.

"Okay, Amanda," she said. "You go get a shovel, and I'll go get some lemonade. I'll meet you back here in a couple minutes."

Amanda went to get a shovel. On the way, she couldn't help thinking that what she *really* wanted was a miracle, not a shovel. But she was thirsty, and she thought she'd enjoy some lemonade while she waited.

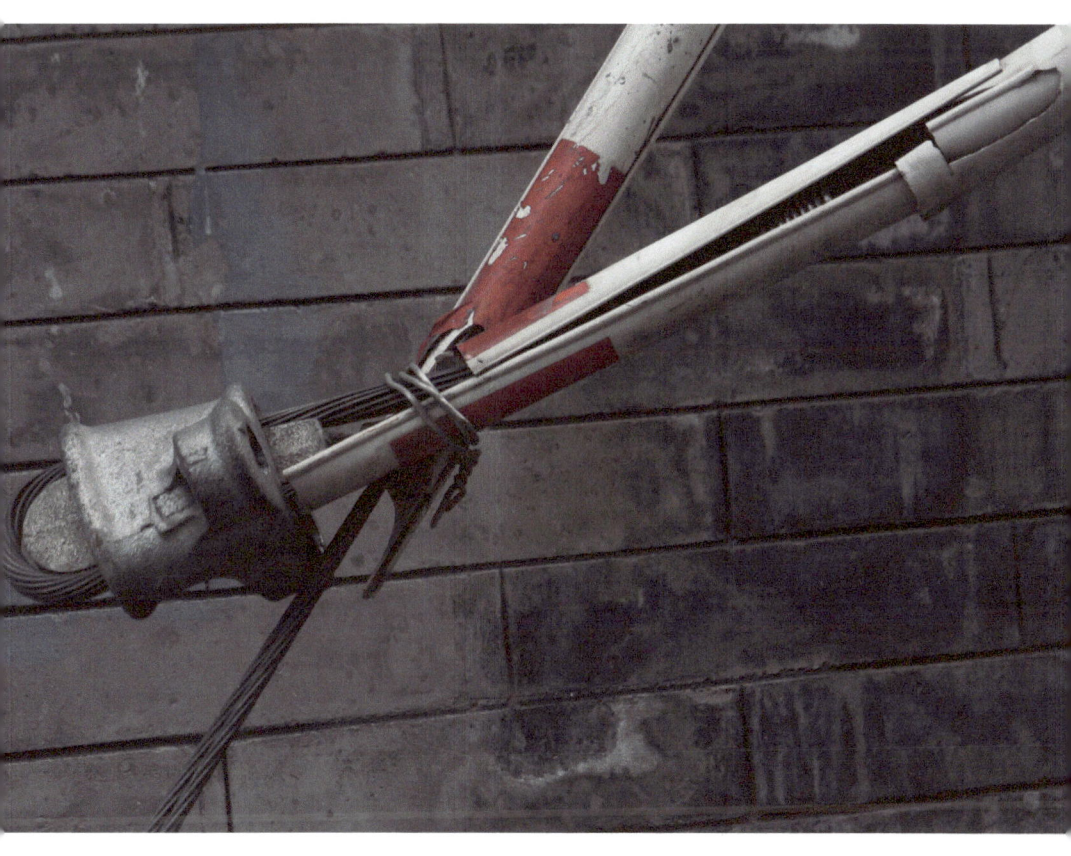

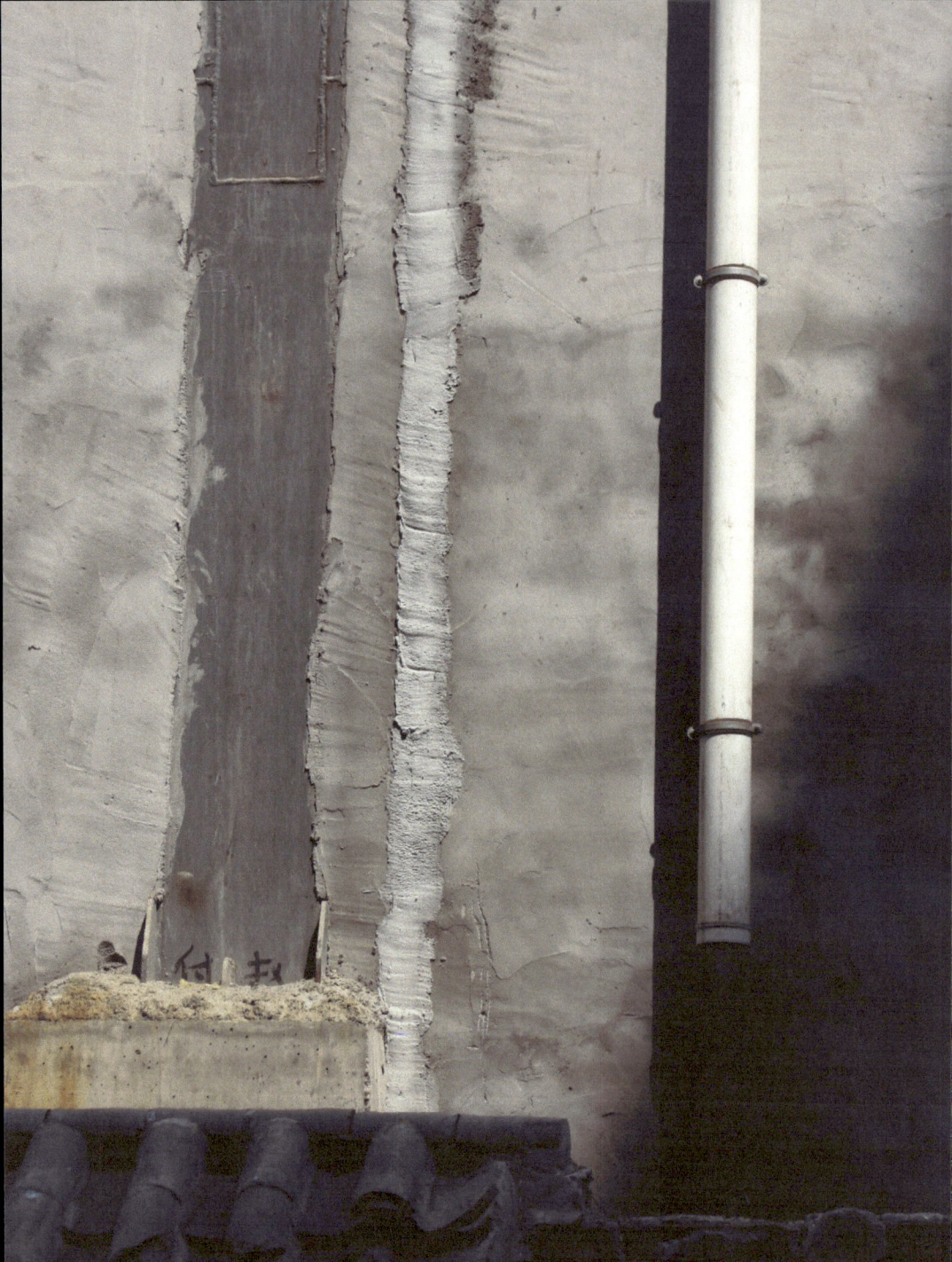

When she got back, her grandmother had put two glasses of ice and a pitcher of lemonade on a small table by two chairs. They sat and sipped lemonade and Amanda told her grandmother all about the miracle she wanted.

When they had each finished two glasses of lemonade, her grandmother said, "Now for the next step. Watch what I do with this shovel." She put one foot on the shovel and stepped on it until it was deep in the dirt. Then she pulled the shovel up. When it was above the ground, she turned the shovel over and let the dirt fall off.

"Now it's your turn, Amanda. Pretend the dirt is a pancake you're going to flip. We want the soil to be nice and loose when we're done."

Flipping dirt pancakes was hard work, and Amanda's grandmother had to help twice before Amanda finished.

Then her grandmother poked three small holes in the ground with her finger and told Amanda to put one seed in each hole. They covered the seeds with soil, and her grandmother stood there, beaming. She brushed the dirt off her hands.

"Well," she said, "That's it. That's how you get a miracle. Unless one falls into your hands, like that pumpkin did earlier."

Amanda tried not to say anything disrespectful. But she couldn't think of anything else, so she just kept quiet. Besides, Amanda thought, maybe it would work. She thanked her grandmother and left to go play.

But the next day? Nothing.

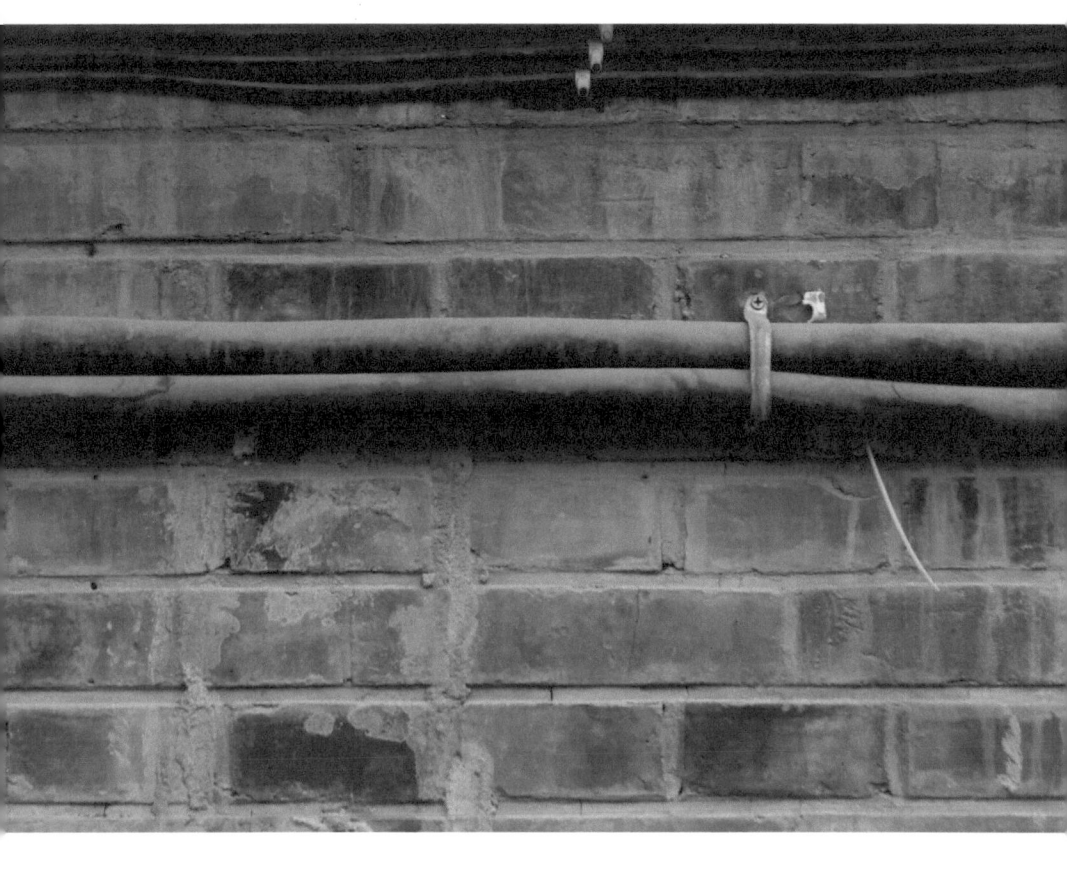

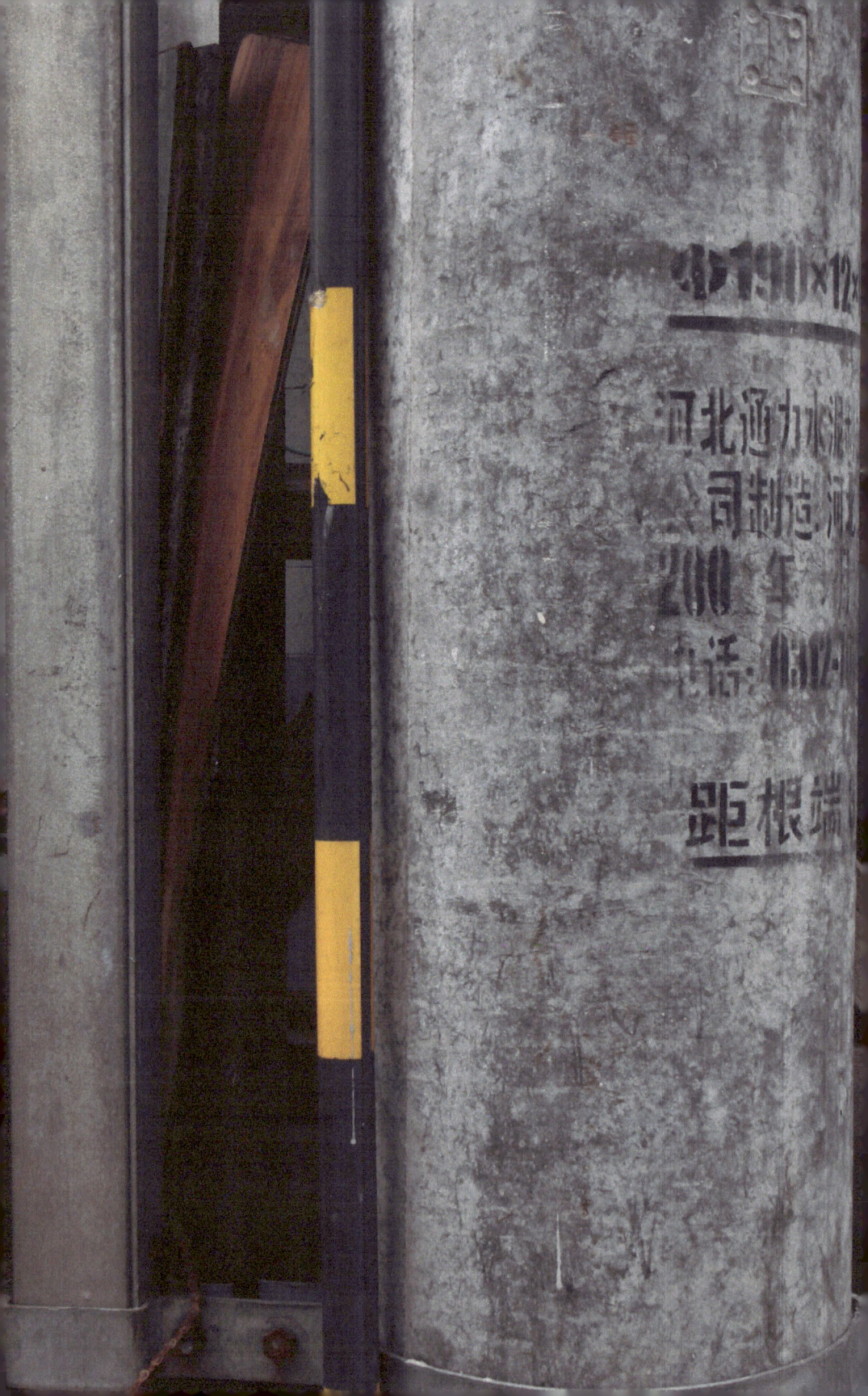

When Amanda woke up the next day, she really expected to have her miracle. Her grandmother had said that planting those seeds was how she'd get it. But Amanda checked everywhere in the house she could think of, and she couldn't find her miracle. At last she remembered to check the garden. But even there: Nothing.

Her grandmother called that afternoon. "I forgot to tell you, dear. You have to water that part of the garden we dug up. Every day. Don't forget – those seeds like to get water."

"*Then* will I get my miracle?" Amanda asked.

"Oh, no, dear," said her grandmother. "You've already gotten your miracle. You just can't see it yet."

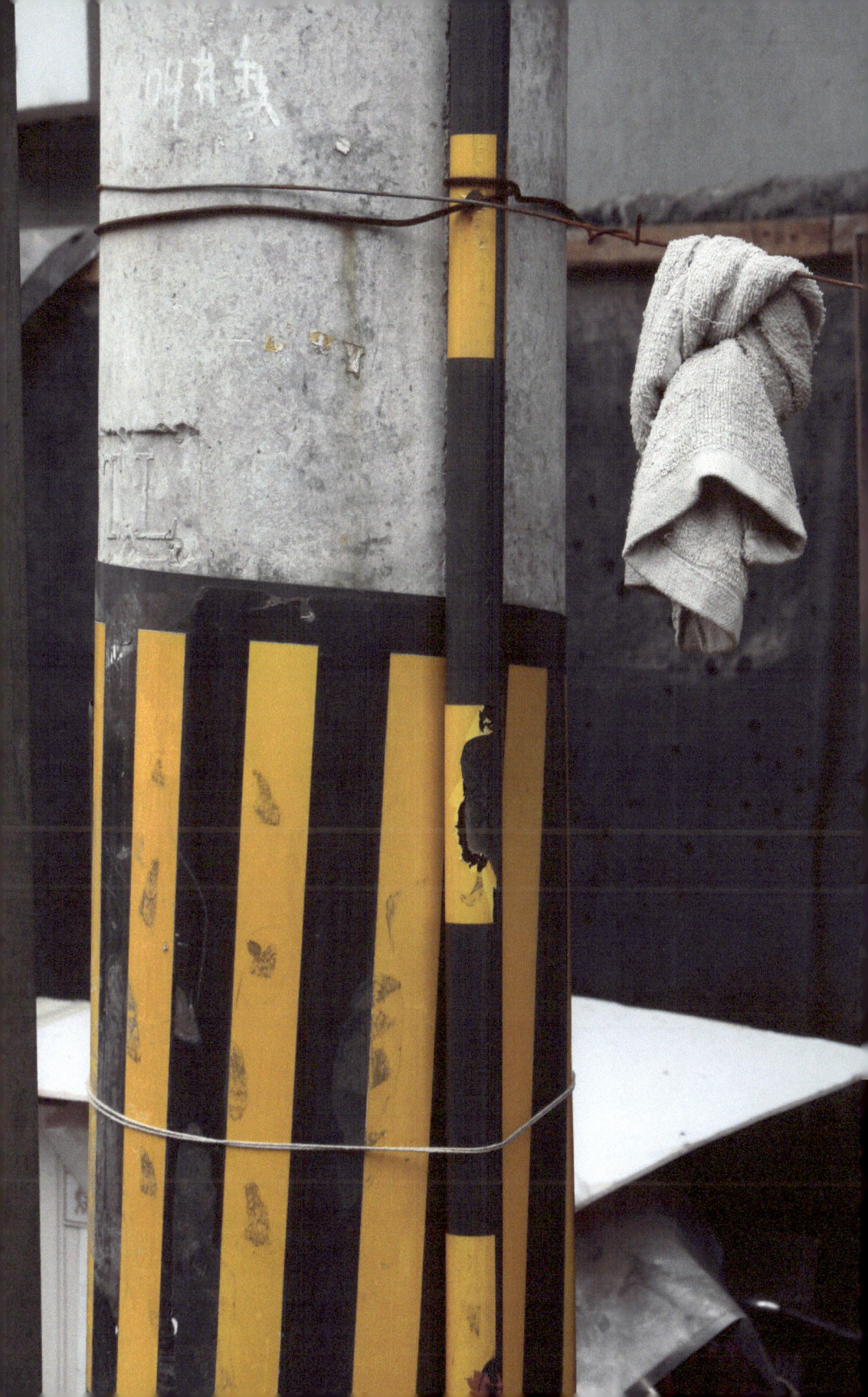

Amanda thought her grandmother made no sense sometimes. But she went out each day and watered the garden, just in case. And each day she looked around the house and yard to see if she could find her miracle. Every day, nothing.

After a week or so, three tiny green plants could be seen in her garden.

Her grandma came to visit fairly often, and each time she visited, they went out to look at the plants. Each day Amanda watered them they got a little bigger.

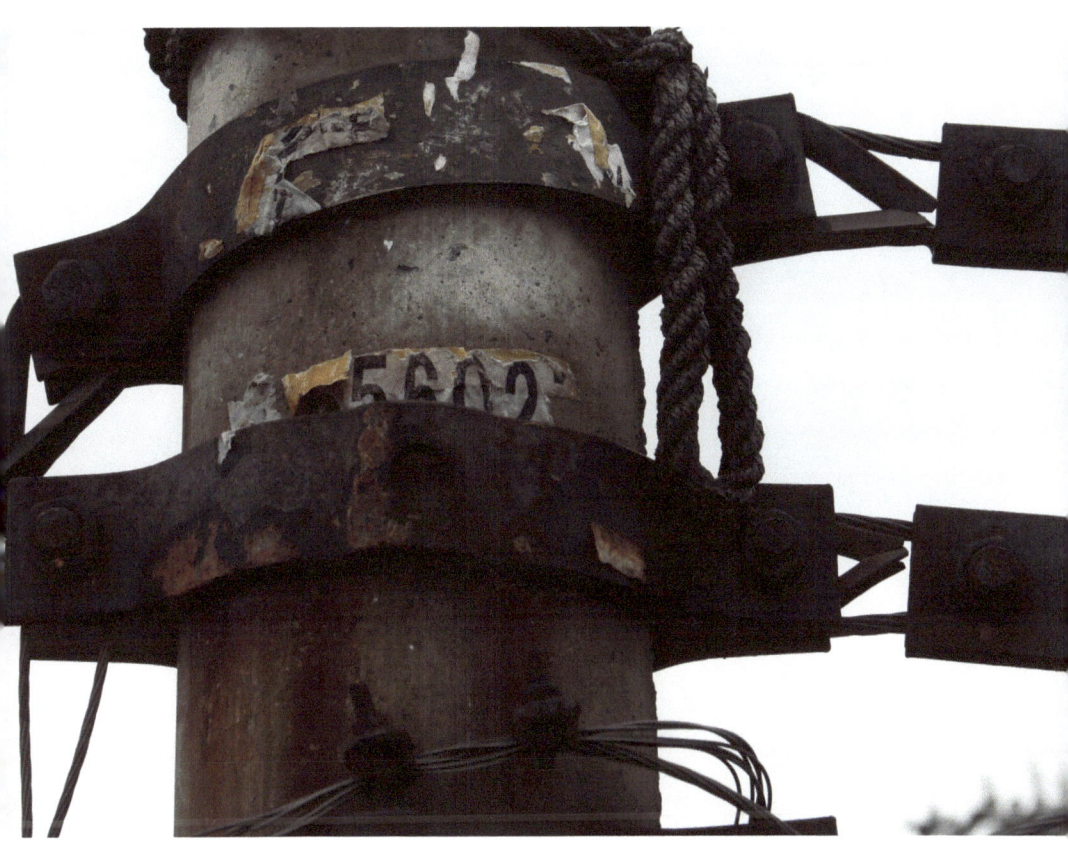

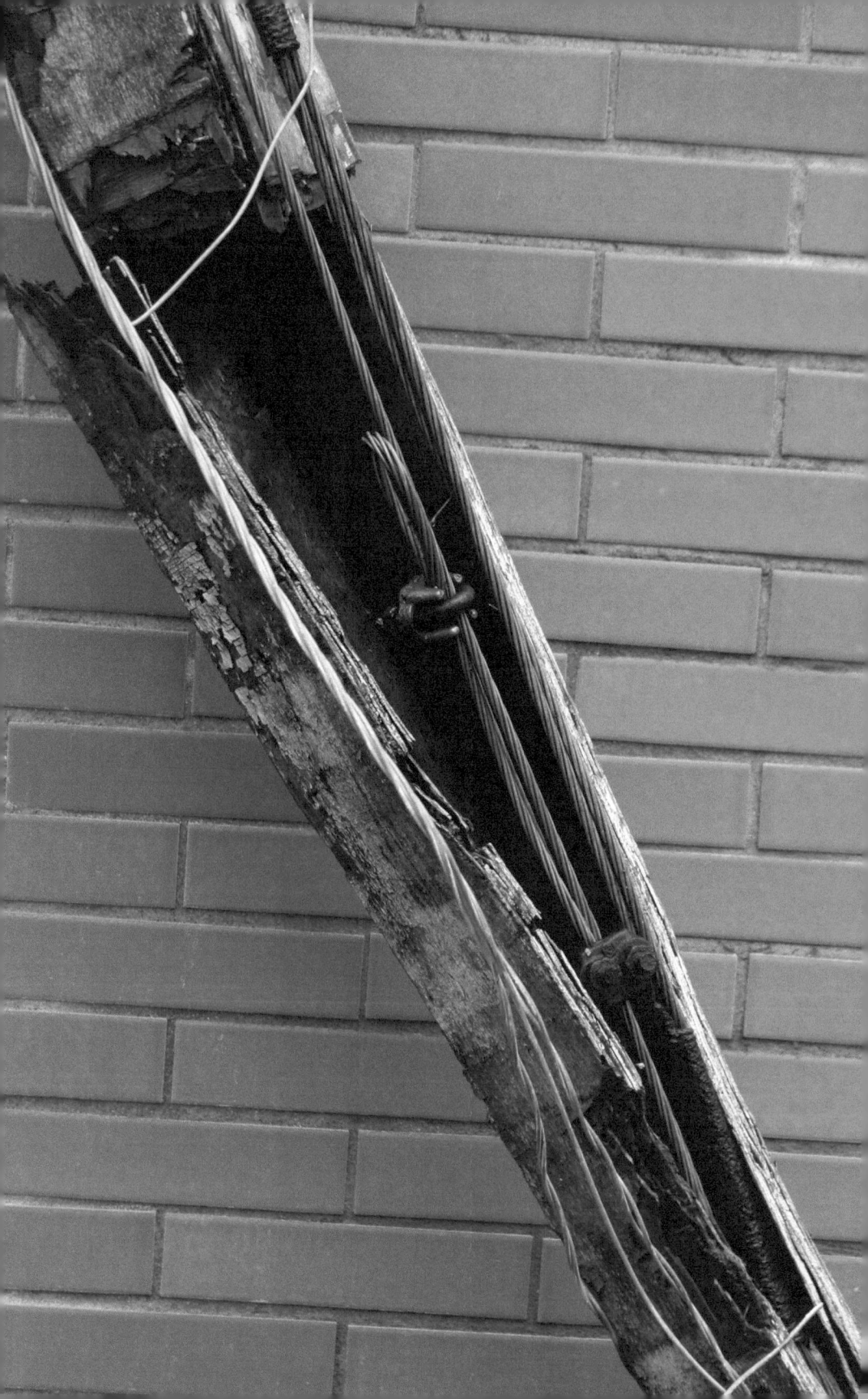

Amanda's grandmother taught Amanda how to fertilize the plants. She taught her which bugs were good, which ones didn't matter, and which bugs would hurt her plants. She taught her how to tell when the plants got sick and what to do about it.

Amanda's grandmother was *very* excited when orange flowers appeared on the plants. She taught Amanda how to attract bees to pollinate the flowers.

Amanda thought the flowers were pretty. They were a very nice color. They had an interesting shape. But she wanted a miracle, not flowers, and certainly not pumpkins. She didn't bring it up, however. Amanda didn't think her grandmother knew very much about miracles. Amanda thought her grandmother was just trying to distract her.

Partly it was working. Between all the watering and fertilizing and spraying and bug watching, Amanda didn't spend too much time wishing for a miracle.

On one of her visits, Amanda's grandmother was excited to see some round bumps on the vines by some of the flowers. The bumps were very small and green, and didn't look that exciting to Amanda. But she tried to smile and be polite.

A month after that, the bumps looked like small pumpkins. A month after that, the small pumpkins looked like medium-sized pumpkins.

Amanda still wanted her miracle, so she kept watering and fertilizing and watching for pests (including her brother) and guarding her plants. The plants were definitely pumpkin plants. They each had several large pumpkins on their vines, and every week the pumpkins grew bigger.

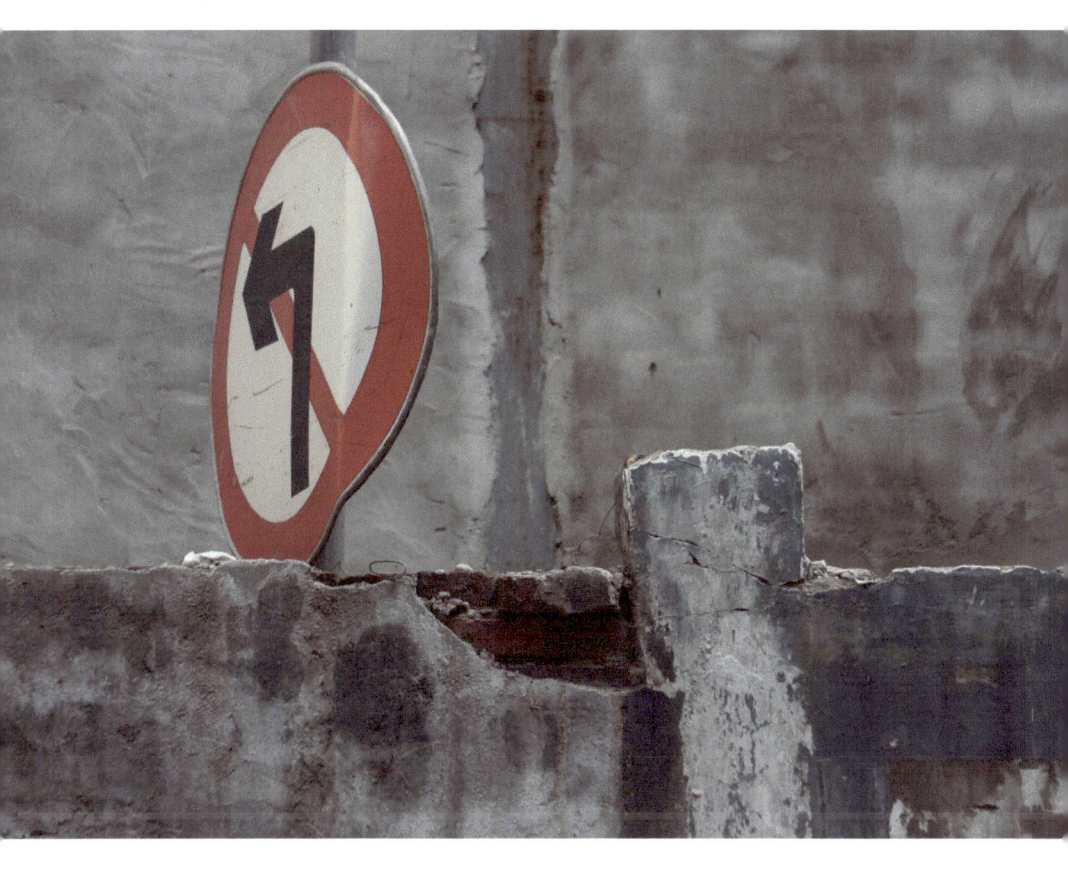

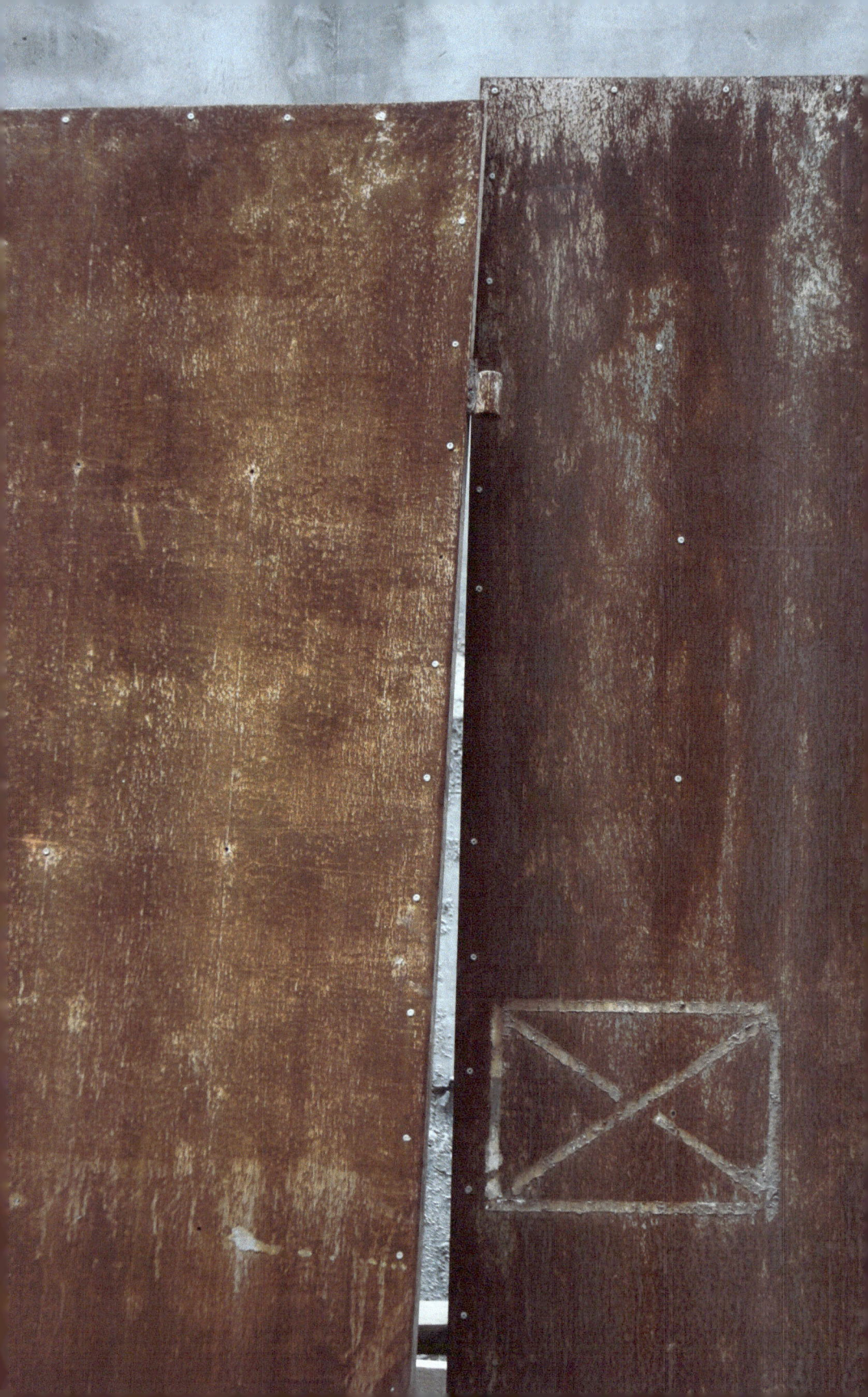

One day, the pumpkins were so big that Amanda's grandmother showed her how to cut them off the vine. Amanda thought she was finally done, but her grandmother said now she had to cure them for a week so their skins would get hard.

A week later her grandmother was visiting and Amanda was playing with her friend Sue. It was nearly Halloween, and Sue saw a picture of a jack-o'-lantern on the door to Amanda's room.

"I wish I had a pumpkin," Sue said.

"Oh!" said Amanda's grandmother, her big eyes twinkling. "Amanda can help you with that! Close your eyes and hold out your hands."

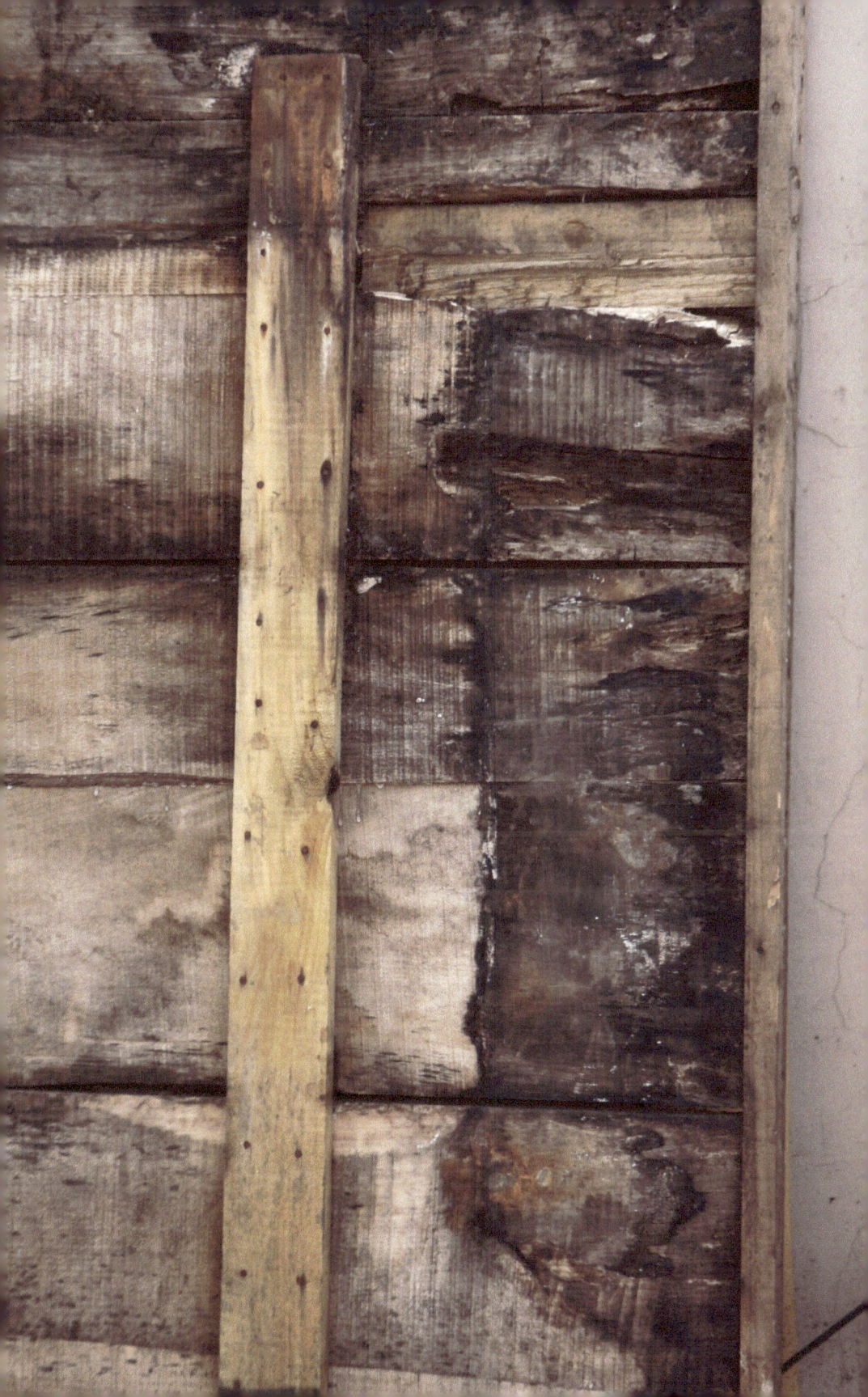

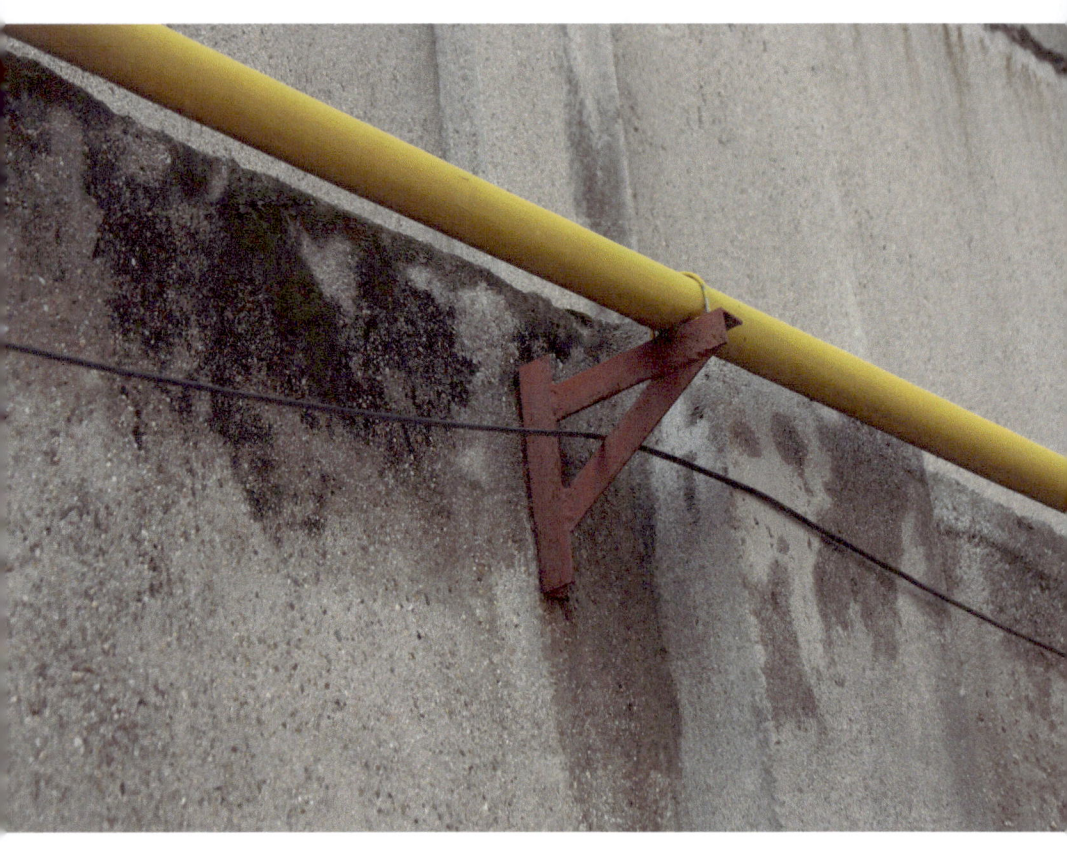

Amanda raced down to the pile of pumpkins and picked out the biggest one she could carry. She climbed back up the stairs to her room and put the pumpkin in her friend's open arms.

Her friend peeked with one eye and then squealed with delight. "Oh!" she said opening both eyes. "Look at that beautiful pumpkin! It's a miracle!"

That night, Amanda's grandma got out some cookies and milk and they sat at the kitchen table, talking.

"There are two ways to get a miracle," said her grandmother. "One way is to ask for it and have someone else do all the hard work."

Amanda liked the sound of that very much.

"That was how Sue got *her* pumpkin," said her grandmother.

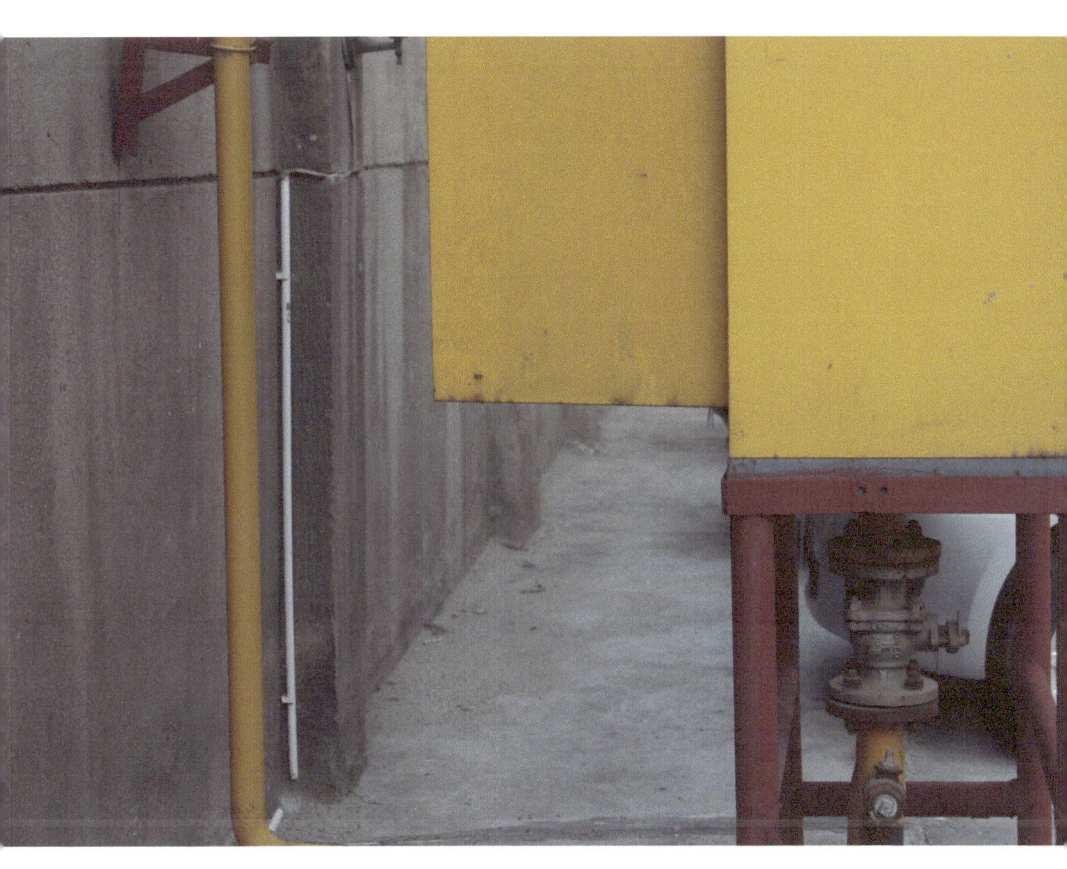

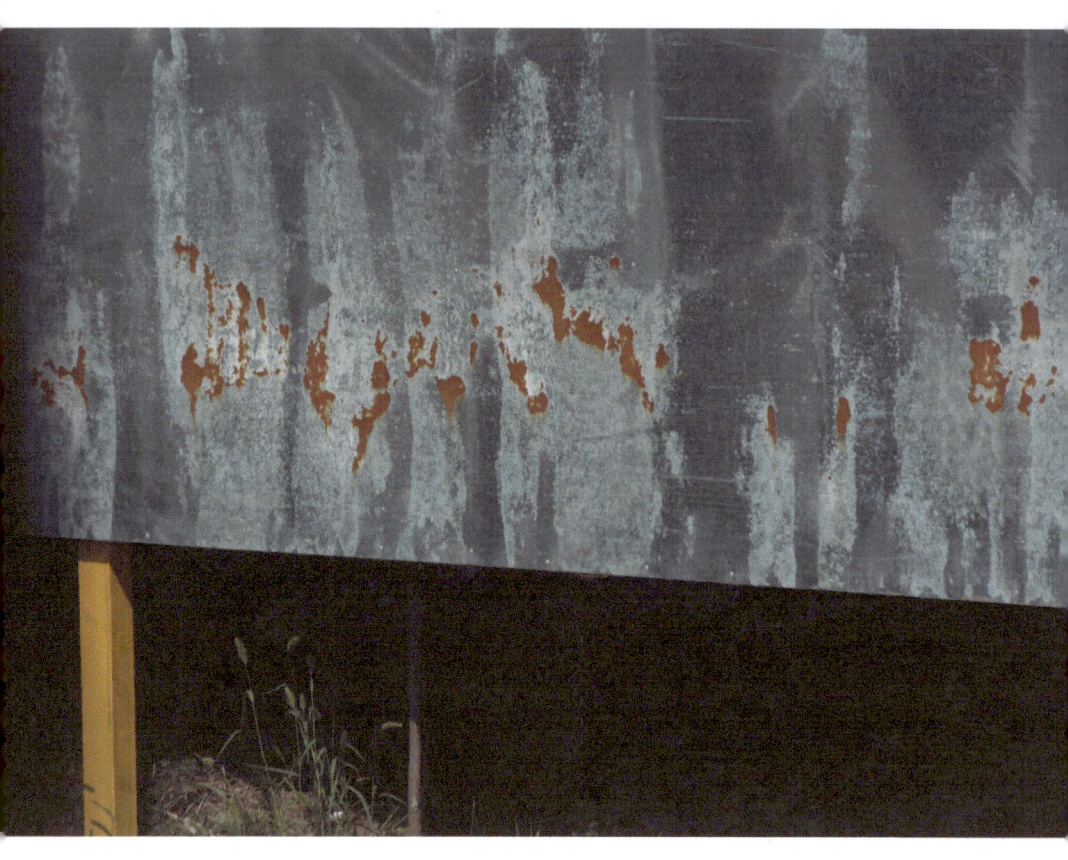

"The other way to get a miracle is to do all the hard work yourself, like you've done the past couple months."

Now that Amanda was sitting in the kitchen eating cookies, she didn't think that raising the pumpkins had really been all that hard.

"The first way *seems* easier," said her grandmother, "and it's great when it happens. But if you do all the hard work yourself, you get more than one pumpkin. It's often better that way."

Amanda definitely had more than one pumpkin. She had a pile of them outside the house. But she really wasn't sure that several pumpkins were better than one.

Her grandmother kissed Amanda on her forehead, and Amanda went off to brush her teeth.

Amanda still wanted her miracle. Maybe, she decided, she'd have to work for it.

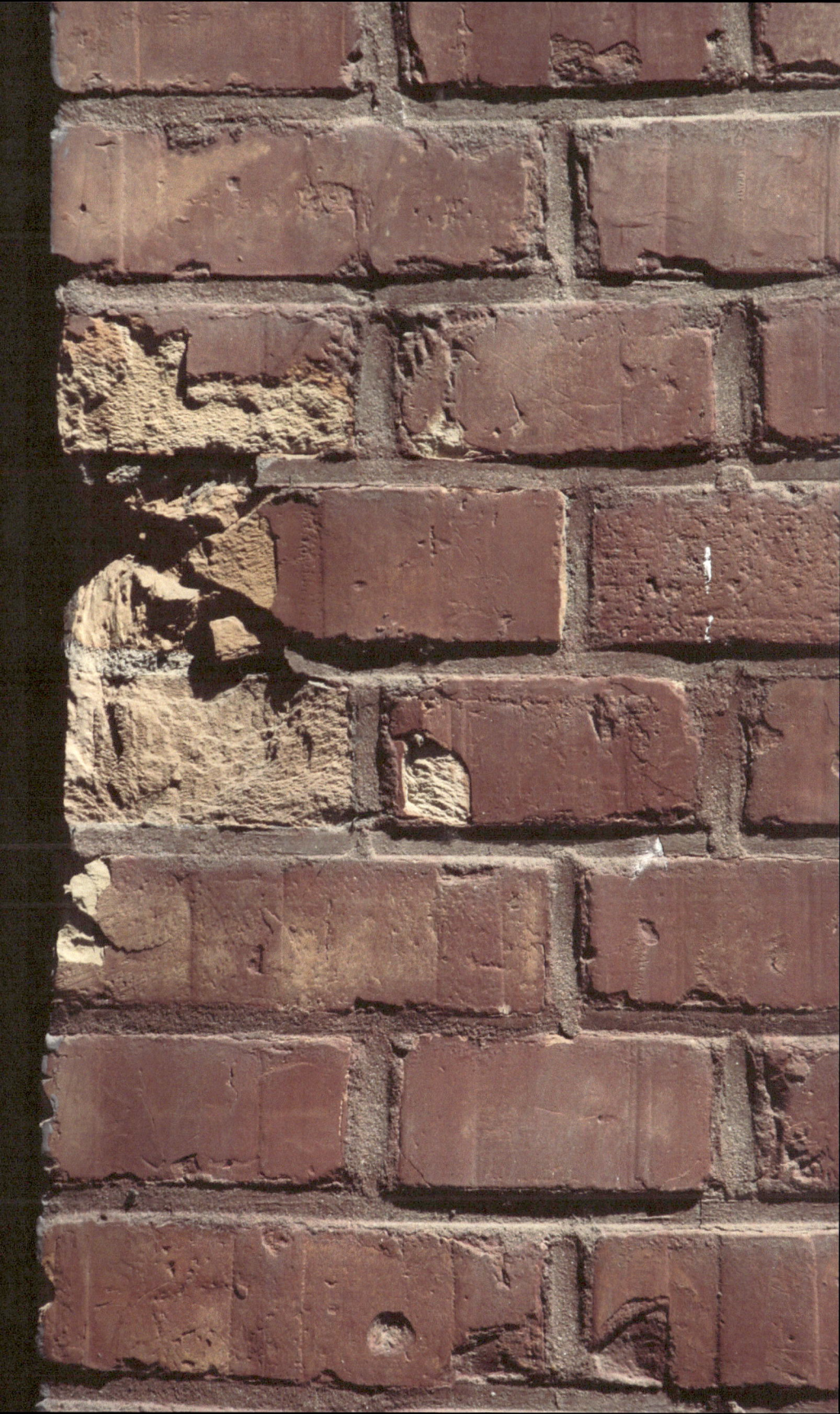

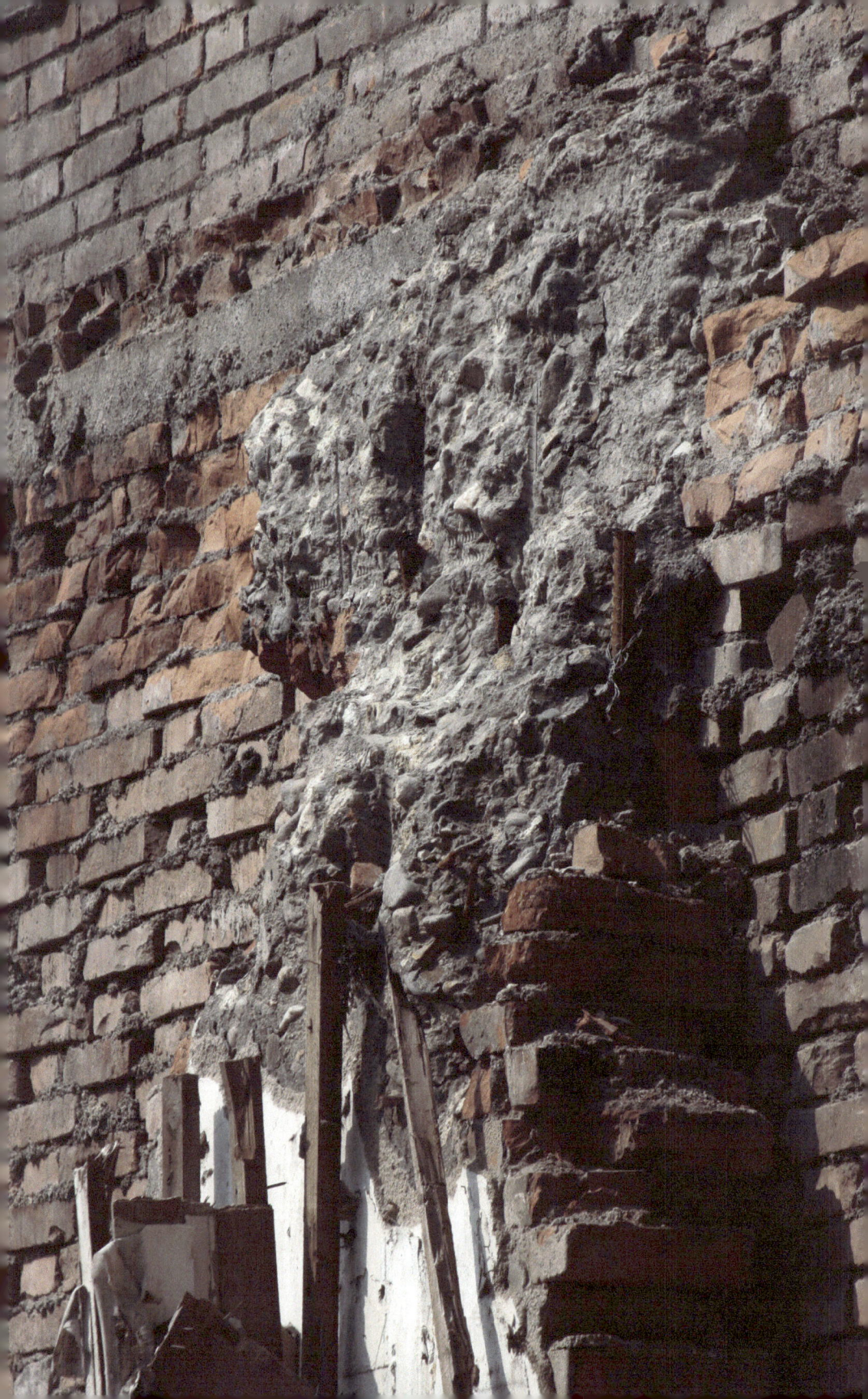

In the kitchen, Amanda's grandmother practiced pulling pumpkins out of thin air and putting them back.

She still had one or two things to teach Amanda. But first Amanda had to learn how to get a miracle by hard work.

~

Reflection Questions

What miracle(s) do you want?

Who could you ask to give you one of your miracles?

What work could you do to get you closer to the miracle(s) you want?

When will you start that work?

~ ~ ~

~ ~ ~

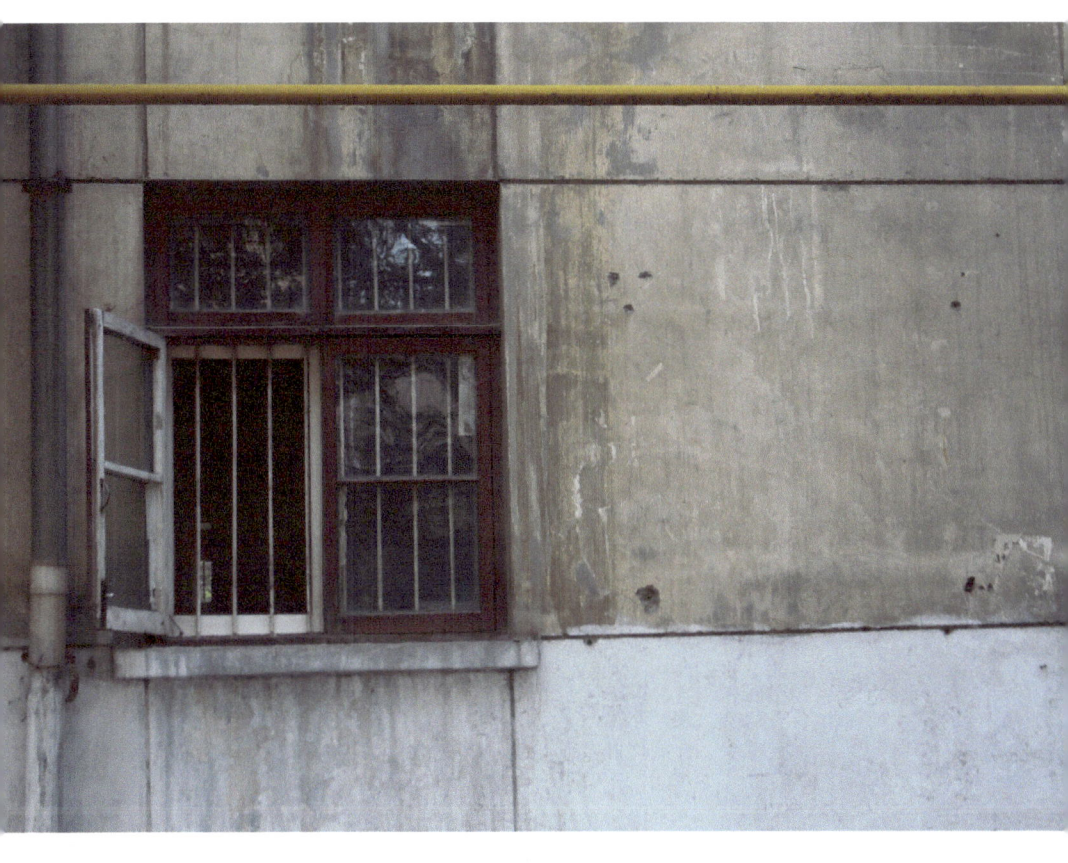

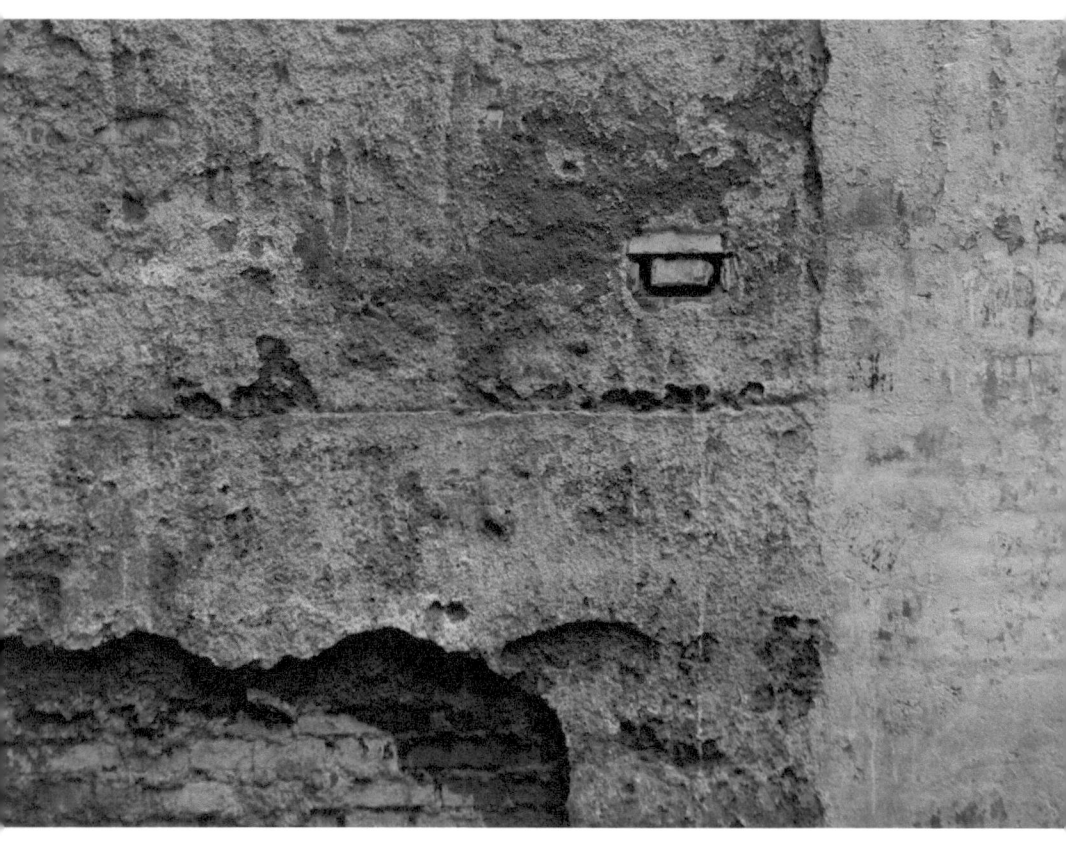

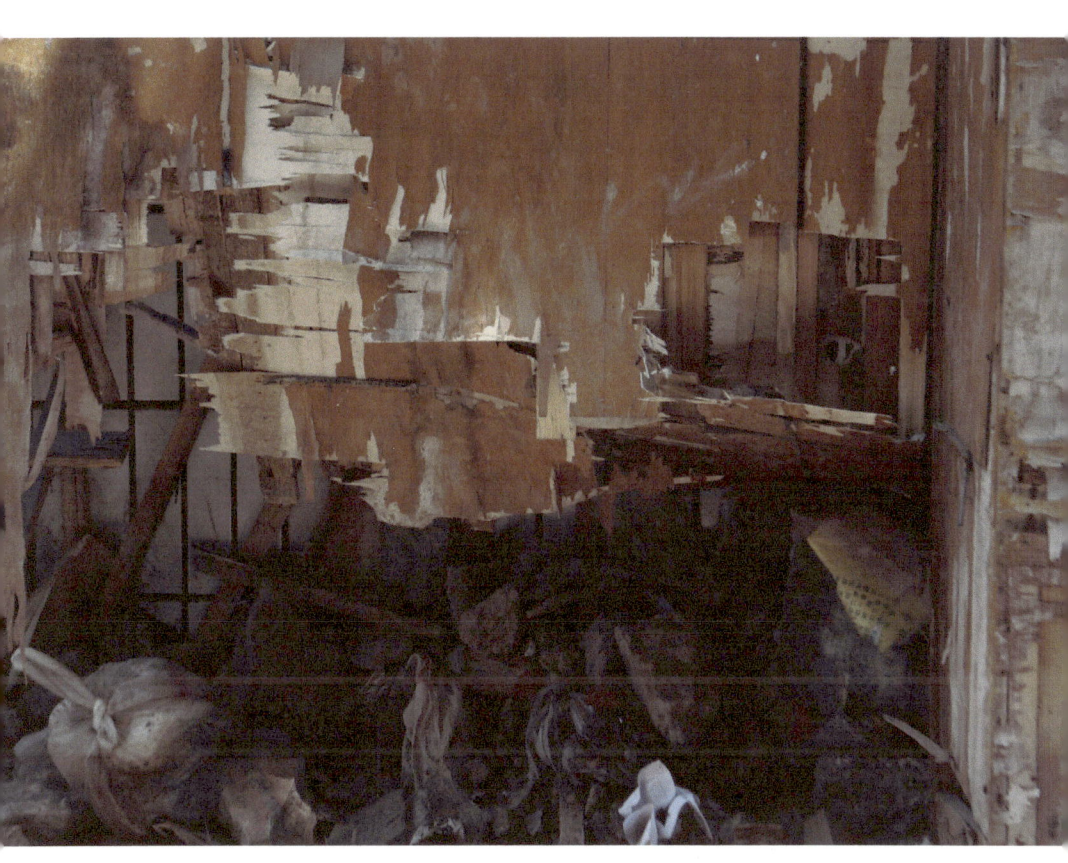

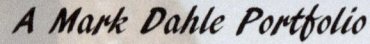

A Mark Dahle Portfolio

Farmer Jane

This Mark Dahle Portfolio includes a beautiful painting, twenty-five gorgeous photographs from the Netherlands, and a story about Farmer Jane.

Jane didn't know that farmers have troubles.

But she was about to discover how *many* troubles they have.

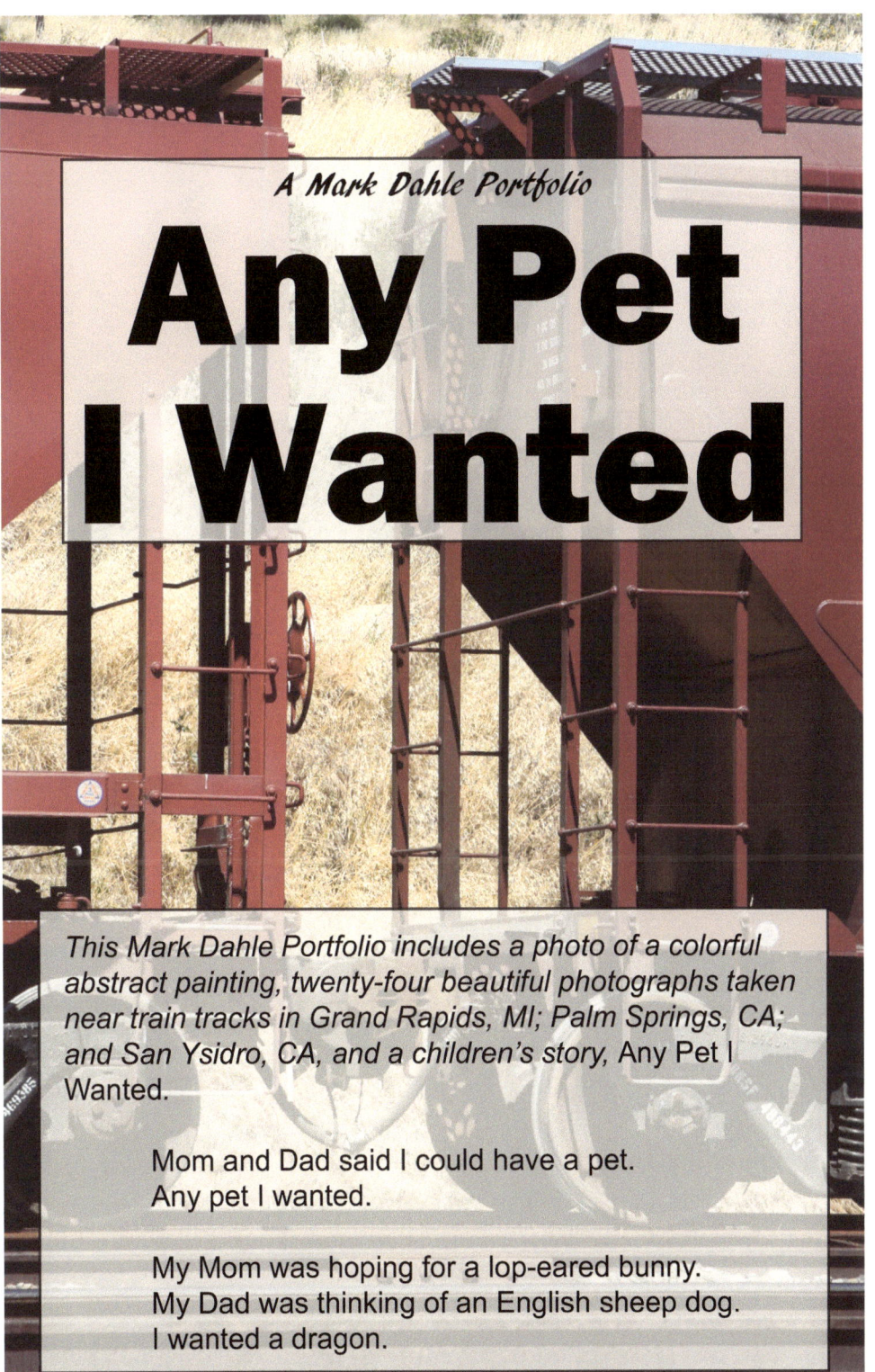

A Mark Dahle Portfolio

Any Pet I Wanted

This Mark Dahle Portfolio includes a photo of a colorful abstract painting, twenty-four beautiful photographs taken near train tracks in Grand Rapids, MI; Palm Springs, CA; and San Ysidro, CA, and a children's story, Any Pet I Wanted.

Mom and Dad said I could have a pet.
Any pet I wanted.

My Mom was hoping for a lop-eared bunny.
My Dad was thinking of an English sheep dog.
I wanted a dragon.

The Boy Who Loved Monopoly

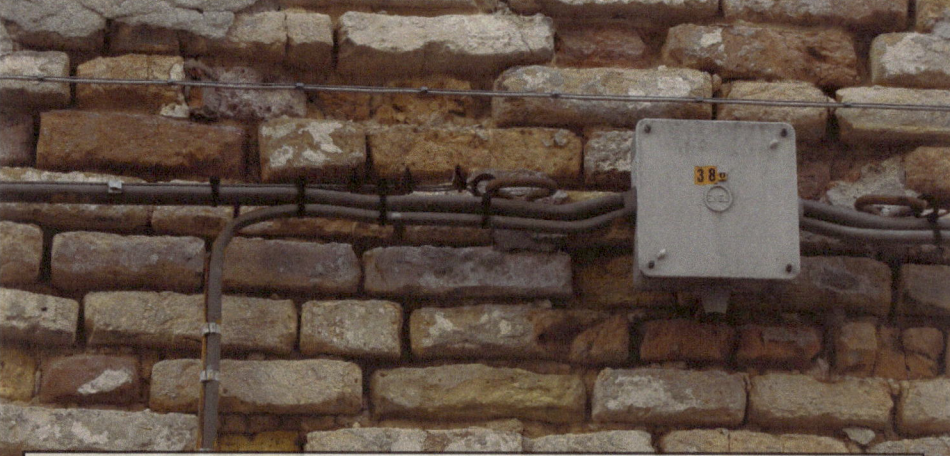

This Mark Dahle Portfolio includes a colorful painting, twenty-seven beautiful photographs of Venice, and a story about a boy who loved to play Monopoly. One day the boy received $250,000 as an inheritance.

You probably haven't inherited any money this week.
But you've got lots of gifts
and lots of things that you're good at –
or could be, after you get more practice.
What will *you* do with all the gifts that *you* have?